What

Story by Joy Cowley • Illustrations by Murray Grimsdale

"What a mess!"
said Auntie Jean.

"I'll fix it all," said Mr. Keen.

3

"I'll fix your stairs,
and I'll fix your chairs.

4

"I'll fix your doors,
and I'll fix your floors.

5

"I'll fix your walls,
and I'll fix your halls.

6

'Help! Help!" said Mr. Keen.

7

"What a mess!"
said Auntie Jean.